MW00947243

GREATER GRACE

21 DEVOTIONS INSPIRED
BY TIMELESS HYMNS

BETHNEY JACOB

WESTBOW
PRESS®
A DIVISION OF THOMAS NELSON
& ZONDERVAN

WestBow Press books may be ordered through booksellers or by contacting:

WestBow Press
A Division of Thomas Nelson & Zondervan
1663 Liberty Drive
Bloomington, IN 47403
www.westbowpress.com
1 (866) 928-1240

ISBN: 978-1-9736-7493-1 (sc)
ISBN: 978-1-9736-7495-5 (hc)
ISBN: 978-1-9736-7494-8 (e)

Library of Congress Control Number: 2019914181

Print information available on the last page.

WestBow Press rev. date: 10/4/2019

CONTENTS

INTRODUCTION

I have always loved hymns. Perhaps it is my love of the written word that draws me to their poetry. Part of the joy of writing this book was discovering unfamiliar hymns and revisiting old favorites. Their lyrics are timeless; expressing truths and experiences which transcend culture and age. There is something about it that ignites the soul. This selection of hymns sparked in me a fresh hunger for God's Word, inspiring these devotional reflections. The heart of this book is best summed up by the Apostle Paul's familiar declaration:

> "I know how to get along and live humbly [in difficult times], and I also know how to enjoy abundance and live in prosperity. In any and every circumstance I have learned the secret [of facing life], whether well-fed or going hungry, whether having an abundance or being in need. *I can do all things* [which He has called me to do] *through Him who strengthens and empowers me* [to fulfill His purpose—I am self-sufficient in Christ's sufficiency; I am ready for anything and equal to anything through Him who infuses me with inner strength and confident peace.]"
> (Philippians 4:12-13 AMP, emphasis mine)

This collection of devotions is a call to grace- to laying down our own assumptions, fears, failures, and boundaries and living in the abundant grace available to us in Christ. I was at first wary to call this a devotional- often that implies a daily reading, which is not necessarily a negative thing, but may not leave room for the mediation and reflection over days and weeks which solidifies our understanding and leads to transformative revelation. I encourage you to throw out your notion of what a devotional is as you read this book. Don't just try to get through it; if something resonates with you, allow yourself to park there for a while. Meditate on the lyrics of the hymn. Read and re-read the scriptures. Look for related scripture. My desire in writing this was to share my own journey of refreshing, repenting, and strengthening as I listened to these hymns and connected them with the truth in God's word. I pray that in these pages we will find shared experiences and you too will be encouraged, challenged, and renewed.

> "I pray that from his glorious, unlimited resources he will empower you with inner strength through his Spirit. Then Christ will make his home in your hearts as you trust in him. Your roots will grow down into God's love and keep you strong. And may you have the power to understand, as all God's people should, how wide, how long, how high, and how deep his love is. May you experience the love of Christ, though it is too great to understand fully. Then you will be made complete with all the fullness of life and power that comes from God. Now all glory to God, who is able, through his mighty power at work within us, to accomplish infinitely more than we might ask or think."
>
> (Ephesians 3:16-19 NLT)

AMAZING GRACE

Lyrics by John Newton (1779)

'Twas grace that taught my heart to fear and grace my fears relieved
How precious did that grace appear the hour I first believed

Read: Titus 3:3-7, 1 Corinthians 1:4-9

Do you remember the moment you accepted Christ? That moment when you realized the crushing reality of your sin and were in awe of the amazing love of Jesus? That moment of joy and rest as you accepted the precious gift of salvation? As Titus 3:3-7 describes, we were truly wretched without Christ, desperately in need of a Saviour. We are saved by grace- the unmerited goodness and love of God; through faith in his Son. God's grace is not a limited offer only available at the time of conversion, however somewhere along the line, the initial reverence and awe that led us to Christ is often replaced by fear, shame, and duty. We put our trust in our own willpower and good works, rather than fearing God.

To fear God is to recognize His holiness- that He is above all, in control of it all, without limits, and incapable of sin or failure. It is a place of humility and peace when we recognize that we cannot do anything without Him (see John 15:5), and through Him we have the power to do anything (see Philippians 4:13). In our own strength we are destined for failure, but God's boundless power is available to those who fear Him: "The Lord watches over those who fear Him, those who *rely on His unfailing love.*" (Psalm 33:18 NLT, emphasis mine) Do we live

1

truly believing God's love will never fail us, or are we working to prove ourselves worthy of His love?

It was in the wonder of God's grace that we initially accepted the gift of salvation. He continues to extend His gift of grace to us so that we may live righteously and purposefully. Let us return to the holy fear that first drew us to the cross, that we would seek Him out of awe and love, recognizing that we are weak, and He is strong: "Continue to *work out your salvation with fear and trembling, for it is God who works in you* to will and to act in order to fulfill his good purpose." (Philippians 2:12b-13 NIV, emphasis mine) This "fear and trembling" does not mean we live in a constant state of anxiety, but rather that we find rest in the realization that we are nothing without Him; that His ways and understanding are far above our ability and comprehension. To "work out our salvation" is not to toil for our salvation, it is working to remain reliant on the grace that first taught us to fear the Lord. It is God who will work in our heart, mind, and circumstances so that His will is accomplished in us and on the earth.

REFLECTION

Are you relying on the love and goodness of God in every area of your life, or are you weary under the weight of striving?

Do you carry the guilt of your mistakes after you have asked the Lord for forgiveness? His forgiveness is sufficient, and He has made us blameless. (see 1 John 1:9)

Are you anxious about your work or ministry? Seek His will in all things, and He will direct your path. We can trust that wherever He leads us is for a purpose and that no season in our life is wasted. (see Jeremiah 29:11-13)

Are you paralyzed by your faults and weaknesses? Do you let opportunities pass you by because you do not feel qualified or worthy? God loves to use those who are "unqualified" and "unimpressive" so that He will ultimately be glorified. If God has called you, you are enough. His grace makes you enough. (see 2 Corinthians 12:9)

Do you refrain from praying bold prayers because you feel they do not deserve to be heard or answered? God has already made the ultimate demonstration of His love for us. His grace and kindness have no limits. He is merciful, and His ear is attentive to our prayers. (see Psalm 66:16-20)

Perhaps you are exhausted by the many responsibilities you have taken on (whether that's in your home, work, relationships, or church). Ask God to show you if these "good works" are things He actually wants you to do. God will give us the wisdom, ability, and strength to work in accordance with His purpose. If our efforts are fuelled by guilt, obligation, or pride, our motive for working is wrong. (see Ephesians 2:8-10)

The grace you received when you first believed is still available to you every day. Repent for the ways you have stopped relying on His grace and commit today to have your mind renewed by His Word. *"He will keep you strong* till the end … for He is faithful to do what He says." (1 Corinthians 1:8-9 NLT, emphasis mine)

NOTES

HOW GREAT THOU ART

Lyrics by Carl Boberg (1885)

And when I think that God, his Son not sparing,
Sent him to die, I scarce can take it in...
Then sings my soul, my Savior God, to thee:
How great thou art!

Read: Psalm 103, Colossians 1:15-20

Holy. Majestic. Sovereign. Awesome. Even these words seem to fall short in capturing our indescribably great God. There is so much to marvel at. The intricacy and order of our bodies, our ecosystems, and the heavens declare the matchless wonder of the Lord. Creation expresses His creativity, His attention to detail, His beauty, His supremacy. When we really begin to ponder these things, we are overwhelmed by our own limits and insignificance. As God reminded Job when he questioned His wisdom:

> "Where were you when I laid the foundations of the earth? Tell me, if you know so much. Who determined its dimensions and stretched out the surveying line? What supports its foundations, and who laid its cornerstone ... Who kept the sea inside its boundaries as it burst from the womb, and as I clothed it with clouds and wrapped it in thick darkness? For I locked it behind barred gates, limiting its shores. I said, 'This far and no farther will

7

you come. Here your proud waves must stop!' Have you ever commanded the morning to appear and caused the dawn to rise in the east? ... Who gives intuition to the heart and instinct to the mind?" (Job 38:4-6, 8-12, 36 NLT)

In light of His power and the vastness of His reign, it is incredible that He sees us and cares for us. We are a speck in the universe, a feather in the weight of all creation; still He knows us each by name. He alone fulfills that deepest longing in the human heart- to be known and understood. Our God is not far off, too busy keeping the planets on their course and seasons on schedule. He does not consider us minutia in His grand design. Our Lord is intimately aware of us: "How precious are your thoughts about me, O God. They cannot be numbered! I can't even count them; they outnumber the grains of sand!" (Psalm 139:17-18 NLT) This is truly amazing to consider- that the Creator and Sustainer of life thinks about us; not as a mass of nameless faces, but as individuals. Even more wondrous is that Jesus would choose to give His life for us. His life was not taken from Him, He gave it freely so that we could not only be known by Him, but that we could know Him- the Father, Son, and Holy Spirit. In His great love, He did not leave us hopelessly lost, but made a way for us to be found in Him. Indeed, how great Thou art.

REFLECTION

Some of us have lost our wonder. When all is well, it is easy to take for granted the ordinary. The sun rises, we wake up, we travel, we eat, we cross paths with others, the sun sets, and we get up and do it all over again tomorrow. Let us not forget that "all things were *created and exist through Him* [that is, by His activity] *and for Him* ... And He Himself existed and is before all things, and *in Him all things hold together.* [*His is the controlling, cohesive force of the universe.*]" (Colossians 1:16-17 AMP, emphasis mine) Our understanding of the solar system, of our bodies, of everything that keeps life humming along should never dampen our awe of the One who made it all. We cannot think that our knowledge of how nature "works" somehow gives us control over it. (It is the Creator Himself who has given us wisdom regarding these things). We could not live a day if not for the grace and goodness of God.

Still, there are others of us that need to be reminded of the depth of His love. He is Lord of all, but that does not mean you have been lost in the crowd. May you know that you are seen by God. There is no where you can go, there is nothing you can do to escape His presence (see Psalm 139:1-16). May He settle in your heart that you are loved. You are not forgotten or forsaken.

We are imbued with purpose; we are made in God's image- there is nothing "ordinary" about our lives! May our wonder never fade- for all that He is, for what He has done, and for who He has made us to be.

NOTES

'TIS SO SWEET TO TRUST IN JESUS

Lyrics by Louisa M.R. Stead (1882)

Just from Jesus simply taking life and rest and joy and peace

Read: Psalm 23

"The Lord is my shepherd (to feed, guide, and shield me). I shall not lack." [Psalm 23:1 AMP] This verse beautifully captures what a shepherd does.

A shepherd makes sure its sheep are provided for. The sheep don't need to scavenge for food or water, nor do they need to store away provisions for times of famine. They trust that their shepherd will take care of them. It would be bizarre for any animal under the care of its master to wander off looking for its own food and water. In the same way, it is senseless for us as God's children to rely on ourselves or others for nourishment. We should live with the expectation that God will provide all our needs, whether that be physical, spiritual, emotional or relational. This provision may appear rather ordinary; not as "miraculous" as manna from Heaven, but we must never take it for granted. It is the Lord who sustains all of His creation: "The eyes of all look to you in hope; you give them their food as they need it. When you open your hand, you satisfy the hunger and thirst of every living thing." (Psalm 145:15-16 NLT)

Although we may not have any first-hand experience with sheep, we can learn a lot about their nature from the Bible. In the many references to sheep throughout God's word, we can see that sheep are prone to stray. They require constant guidance. For example, before His arrest,

Jesus quoted what was prophesied in the book of Zephaniah regarding His disciples, saying "God will strike the Shepherd, and the sheep of the flock will be scattered." (Matthew 26:31 NLT) Without a shepherd, sheep will leave the safety of the flock and be lost. After His arrest and crucifixion, Jesus' disciples went into hiding and refused to believe that Jesus had risen from the dead (see John chapter 20). Without their leader, they became cowardly and filled with doubt. The Good Shepherd guides us into all truth- first the truth of the Gospel, and then into right living as we continue to follow Him.

Shepherds must be prepared to risk their life for the safety of their flock. When the angel appeared to the shepherds to announce the Messiah's birth, they were guarding their flock at night (see Luke 2:8). A competent shepherd ensures that no predator will kill the sheep. The prophet Isaiah compares the sinful leaders of Israel to shepherds, condemning them for their negligence. They are examples of ineffective shepherds- they had allowed God's people to fall into sin: "Come, wild animals of the field! Come, wild animals of the forest! Come and devour my people! For the leaders of my people—the Lord's watchmen, his shepherds—are blind and ignorant. They are like silent watchdogs that give no warning when danger comes. They love to lie around, sleeping and dreaming … They are ignorant shepherds, all following their own path and intent on personal gain." (Isaiah 56:9-11 NLT) Unlike Israel's careless and selfish leaders, Jesus- our Good Shepherd, made the ultimate demonstration of His love and care for us. He left the glory of Heaven and died a brutal death so that we would be free from sin and have an eternal, abundant life. He ensured we would not be devoured by the evil one, and instead live in the bliss of His presence forever.

As one in the flock of our Lord and Savior, there is no lack in our lives. What a sweet promise! We can trust the Shepherd of our souls to meet our every need. As we rely on Him, we will experience joyous rest and life-giving hope.

REFLECTION

Where is there lack in your life? Our Lord cares about all our needs, big or small. You have all that you need in our Good Shepherd, Jesus Christ. Perhaps you have strayed from the flock and gone your own way and He is pursuing you. Perhaps you are searching for sustenance- all the while God holds out His hand of love and abundance toward you, patiently waiting. Or maybe you are in danger and in need of rescue- God is attentively awaiting your cry. As you trust and rely on Him, you will experience the sweet joy and peace that only He can bring.

NOTES

IN CHRIST ALONE

Lyrics by Keith Getty, Stuart Townend (2001)

No guilt in life, no fear in death,
This is the power of Christ in me
From life's first cry to final breath,
Jesus commands my destiny ...
Here in the power of Christ I'll stand.

Read: Judges 6, 7:1-22

The account of Gideon in Judges chapters 6-8 is one of the countless times God used one willing person to rescue His people and bring glory to Himself. The Israelites had (once again) turned away from the Lord, and as a result, God allowed the Midianites to strip Israel of everything. (Judges 6:1-6) We meet Gideon threshing wheat at the bottom of a winepress in hope that he will not be discovered by the Midianites. The angel of the Lord greets him saying "Mighty hero, the Lord is with you!" (Judges 6:12 NLT) Gideon is neither mighty nor heroic, but God calls out His purpose for Gideon before it is accomplished. God knows that He has designed Gideon for greatness, even though by human standards, he is unimportant and uncertain of himself. Gideon is from the weakest clan and is the "least" in his family. (Judges 6:15) His faith is small- he asks the Lord for three signs as proof of God's identity and ability before he is ready to go to battle. However, Gideon fears God. When he realizes he has seen an angel of the Lord, he cries out: "Oh, Sovereign Lord, I'm doomed! I have seen the angel of the Lord face to face!" (Judges 6:22 NLT) He immediately obeys when the Lord tells him to destroy the altar and idol in his father's house and build an altar to the one true God. Gideon recognizes the holiness and majesty of God; he regards Him with the honour and reverence He deserves.

God uses an ordinary and rather unimpressive man, a very unconventional battle strategy (Judges 7:15-22), and ridiculously unfavourable odds (Israel's army was outnumbered at least 450:1- see Judges 8:10) to rescue Israel and remind His people who is truly God. Gideon's story beautifully demonstrates the words of Paul in 1 Corinthians 1:24-29:

> "But to those called by God to salvation, both Jews and Gentiles, Christ is the power of God and the wisdom of God. This foolish plan of God is wiser than the wisest of human plans, and *God's weakness is stronger than the greatest of human strength.* Remember, dear brothers and sisters, that few of you were wise in the world's eyes or powerful or wealthy when God called you. Instead … *He chose things that are powerless to shame those who are powerful* … As a result, *no one can ever boast* in the presence of God." (NLT, emphasis mine)

Perhaps we know intellectually that God does not work within the bounds of what is reasonable and natural, but for most of us it is difficult to truly stand "in the power of Christ." It is Christ's power that has saved us from our sins and given us hope of eternal life, but we have been saved for so much more than just entrance into Heaven. God is calling each of us into a divine purpose that transcends our perceived talents and abilities. Our purpose is not determined by our IQ, family, culture, charisma, education, wealth, status, or athleticism. It is determined only by our answer to His call.

REFLECTION

Where does your confidence lie? Has God asked you to do something that seems impossible or unreasonable to you? Just as God made a way for our salvation through Jesus Christ- we could not save ourselves; it is His supernatural power and wisdom that will accomplish His will in us. God is not calling us to muster up the strength and resources to carry out His purpose for our lives; in fact, He delights in using us in the most unexpected and unnatural ways. God is asking you to "Go with the strength you have." (Judges 6:14 NLT) As feeble as that strength may be, if you are willing to put your confidence in the Lord, you will find success: "I [the Lord] will be with you. And you will destroy the Midianites as if you were fighting against one man." (Judges 6:16 NLT)

NOTES

RESCUE THE PERISHING

Lyrics by Fanny Crosby (1869)

Rescue the perishing,
Care for the dying,
Snatch them in pity from sin and the grave;
Weep o'er the erring one,
Lift up the fallen,
Tell them of Jesus the mighty to save.

Read: Luke 7:36-50, Luke 15:1-10

"Compassion" and "empathy" have become buzz words in our western culture; "giving back" is upheld as proof of a person's morality and humanity, and within the church it is considered an imperative. While these pursuits certainly bless those in receipt of our philanthropic efforts, the culture of a "cause" has the potential to create a chasm between the giver and recipient; an "us" and "them" mentality, which gives us a false sense of righteousness. It is far simpler to stand behind a counter serving food or organizing donations; far more comfortable to limit our compassion to giving to the stranger on the street, making small talk with the neighbour across the road, and being friendly to the cashier at the store than it is to invite "them" into our lives. These things are all good and necessary, but it cannot be the whole of our efforts. Jesus taught crowds of people, he healed many as he traveled and then sent them on their way, but that was not where his ministry ended. He spent quality time with sinners:

"As Jesus was walking along, he saw a man named Matthew sitting at his tax collector's booth. 'Follow me and be my disciple,' Jesus said to him. So, Matthew got up and followed him. Later, Matthew invited Jesus and his disciples to his home as dinner guests, along with many tax collectors and other disreputable sinners. But when the Pharisees saw this, they asked his disciples, 'Why does your teacher eat with such scum?" (Matthew 9:9-12 NLT)

The Pharisees' response exposes a heart of discrimination and conceit. According to the Pharisees, some people are not deserving of our love and kindness. The act of entering someone's home, of sharing a meal says- I see you, I want to know you, you are important. Jesus illustrates in the parables of the lost sheep and the lost coin that everyone is precious and worthy of time and attention. No one searches earnestly for what is worthless and useless. In the kingdom of God there is no person who has been written off; He came to rescue all (see John 3:16). John 3:16 is a familiar verse, perhaps one of the first verses we committed to memory as Christians; but if we really took it to heart, we would not insulate ourselves from sinners. His love and mercy are not just for us, but it is for the whole world. Salvation is not just for us who believe, it is for all who believe. We often forget that we were once just like "them", and if not for the Lord, we would still be lost. Jesus observes this prideful attitude in Simon the Pharisee's reaction toward the lavish actions of a sinful woman. To Simon she is "a [notorious] sinner [an outcast, devoted to sin]" (Luke 7:39, AMP), but Jesus commends the woman because He recognizes her heart of love and repentance. The Lord "will not reject a broken and repentant heart" (Psalm 51:17 NLT). We came to Him in filthy rags, marred by sin. He made us spotless and blameless. We should recognize that He has the same desire for every person, and we should desperately want everyone to experience His precious gift of salvation.

REFLECTION

We may have accepted Christ as a child and followed Him faithfully all our life. Or perhaps we came to salvation later in life and can vividly recall our waywardness. Either way, we cannot boast in our righteousness. We have right standing with God because of what Christ did for us on the cross. We have made it this far in our walk with the Lord because of His mercy and faithfulness, not because we are spiritually superior. Who knows what trajectory our life would have taken if we were born into a different family, in a different generation, or in a different part of the world? We need to stop seeing people outside our circle as a "cause"; a box to check off on our list of Christian duties and move toward seeing people as God's beloved- perhaps a bit messy, but aren't we all? They are just as loved by God as we are. If we truly have received the ultimate gift, our hearts would break for those who have yet to take hold of it. The investment of our time and heart and the sometimes uncomfortable feeling of fellowshipping with those who share a very different world view than us would not be an inconvenience and a burden. Instead, it would be a joy and privilege to invite them into our lives and into our homes:

> *"Christ's love controls us ...* He died *for everyone* so that those who receive his new life will no longer live for themselves. Instead, they will live for Christ, who died and was raised for them. *So we have stopped evaluating others from a human point of view.* At one time we thought of Christ merely from a human point of view. How differently we know him now! And all of this is a

gift from God, who brought us back to himself through Christ. *And God has given us this task of reconciling people to him … So we are Christ's ambassadors; God is making his appeal through us. We speak for Christ when we plead, 'Come back to God!'"* (2 Corinthians 5:14-20 NLT, emphasis mine)

This is our mandate. And it is ultimately inspired not by obligation or pride, but by love, kindness, and a thankful heart.

NOTES

I NEED THEE EVERY HOUR

Lyrics by Annie S. Hawks, Robert Lowry (1872)

I need thee every hour,
In joy or pain.
Come quickly and abide,
Or life is vain ...
Oh, bless me now, my Savior;
I come to thee!

Read: Jeremiah 17:5-8, Psalm 1

Often in church and Christian circles we hear about being "blessed". Usually the blessings from God that we talk about, pray about, and expect are that of material provision, protection, health, status, healthy relationships, and general personal comfort. Of course, there is nothing inherently wrong with this view. We are to rely on the Lord to meet all our needs and fulfill our heart's desires. But what happens when we aren't healed? Or we remain unemployed? Where is the blessing in broken relationships and lost loved ones? Jesus said, "Blessed are those who mourn, for they will be comforted." (Matthew 5:4 NIV) How is this possible? There are blessings available to us that are not found in temporary comforts and fleeting joys. God offers us sweeter, higher blessings than anything we seek here on earth.

Both Psalm 1 and Jeremiah 17:5-8 contrast those who will be blessed and those who are under a curse. As with many of the promises in God's

25

word, our receiving of the blessing is conditional. There are many good things available to us, but we must choose to take hold of them:

> "I call heaven and earth as witnesses against you today, that *I have set before you life and death, the blessing and the curse; therefore, you shall choose* life in order that you may live … by loving the Lord your God, by obeying His voice, and by *holding closely to Him; for He is your life [your good life, your abundant life, your fulfillment]* and the length of your days." (Deuteronomy 30:19-20 AMP, emphasis mine)

God spoke these words through Moses to the Israelites just before they entered the Promised Land. The Lord fulfilled the promise He made to Abraham when His descendants entered the Promised Land; and He fulfilled His promise of a Savior when He sent Jesus as the sacrifice for the sins of the world. Just as the Israelites entered that Promised Land; we have entered a relationship with God through our faith in Jesus Christ. How we live in this new "Promised Land" is our choice. There are those of us who are satisfied with labeling ourselves as Christians- we believe in Christ and we have accepted His gift of salvation, but we are not expecting or experiencing the abundance of spiritual blessings that are available to us. When trials come, when people disappoint us, when prayers seem to go unanswered, or we struggle to hear from God; we become disillusioned and filled with self pity: "like stunted shrubs in the desert, with no hope for the future." (Jeremiah 17:6 NLT) We can choose to simply survive- still technically alive (by grace, through faith in Christ), but our faith remaining small; our growth constantly curtailed by our feelings and circumstances. Or we can choose to thrive: "They are like trees planted along a riverbank, with *roots that reach deep into the water.* Such trees are not bothered by the heat or worried by long months of drought. *Their leaves stay green, and they never stop producing fruit.*" (Jeremiah 17:8 NLT, emphasis mine) The person who is fruitful in every season is connected to the ultimate source of nourishment and refreshing. This person " …delights in the law of the Lord, meditating on it *day and night.*" (Psalm 1:2 NLT, emphasis mine) Our spiritual growth and the presence of good fruit in our lives (see Galatians 5:22-23) is a direct result of how much time and energy we put into remaining connected to our source- Jesus Christ. An intimate, vibrant, life-transforming relationship with God will not occur unless we are perpetually refreshing our souls so that our roots may grow deep in Him.

Whether we are in a season of life that is exciting, monotonous, or painful; we can abound in the blessings of God. God will bless us with many possessions, relationships, and roles in this life, but none of it will last forever. The blessings of love, rest, joy, faith, hope, wisdom, peace, and self control are eternal and independent of our circumstances.

REFLECTION

Perhaps after reading this you are encouraged to deepen your relationship with God, but you are unsure how to make it happen. God's word says that His mercies are new each morning (see Lamentation 3:22-23). That means that every day we have a fresh opportunity to choose life. Don't become overwhelmed by your weaknesses and shortcomings. Leave the past behind you, trust God with the future, and focus on what you have today. Habits are developed by daily choices. God will give you sufficient strength and wisdom for each day as it comes; you only need to choose His presence.

Often, we wait until there is some tangible need in our lives before we fervently seek God's blessings. May we instead desire those blessings which are everlasting and seek God earnestly each day. As days turn into months and years, the choices we make each day ultimately become our fate. May we choose the abundant life Christ died for us to have.

NOTES

WHAT A FRIEND WE
HAVE IN JESUS

Lyrics by Joseph Medlicott Scriven (1855)

Can we find a friend so faithful,
Who will all our sorrows share?
Jesus knows our every weakness;
Take it to the Lord in prayer.

Read: Matthew 26:31-55

It may be easy for many of us to think of God as our King, our Saviour, our Provider, the Holy One; but our Friend? That is a title with implications of intimacy and shared experience which is often difficult to comprehend. Even though we may not intend to, we tend to try and hide our "ugly" emotions and our deepest scars from God. Perhaps we are ashamed of how we feel. Perhaps we fear God is tired of hearing from us about the same issues. We mask our struggles and feign strength. Whatever the reason, the intimacy of friendship with Jesus cannot be experienced when we are dishonest with ourselves and with Him.

Those final hours before Jesus' arrest were perhaps the darkest moments of His life on earth. Jesus tells his friends "My soul is crushed with grief to the point of death." (Matthew 26:38 NLT) Have you ever been so low you felt like you were dying? God has. Jesus did not try to put on a brave face and move on. He goes off by himself to pray and pours out his heart: "My Father! If it is possible, let this cup of suffering be taken away from me." (Matthew 26:39a NLT) Jesus cries out to the Father- please find another way to save them, I don't want to go through this agony! He is vulnerable and candid. For many of us (especially those of us who have been steeped in church culture for much of our lives) we have learned that our "negative" emotions are a hindrance to our walk with God. There is a sense that we should rally and rise to the occasion regardless of how we feel. By the power of God, our feelings do not need to dictate the trajectory of our lives; but there is a difference between pressing forward in spite of our emotions and pressing forward by numbing our emotions. The former is done through the power of the Sprit of God- when we run into the arms of our Savior with our fears, anger, frustration, shame, and sorrow and allow Him to strengthen, guide, and heal us. The latter is done in our own strength and requires us turn to unhealthy sources of relief so that we can keep moving forward- this will eventually lead to burnout and bitterness; and often feeds patterns of unhealthy behaviour.

Jesus ultimately says to his Father "…I want your will to be done, not mine." (Matthew 26:39b NLT) Despite the overwhelming weight of sorrow, Jesus does His Father's will. We too can do this. Jesus is God- the Holy One, the Mighty King, the Awesome Savior. The beauty of Jesus coming to earth as fully God and fully man is that He is truly the only friend we have who has the power to rescue us from the darkness in this world and who has personally grappled with that darkness himself. Jesus understands immense physical suffering. He knows what it is to be betrayed, abandoned, and ridiculed. (see Matthew 26 and 27) Not only can we trust the power and sovereignty of God; we can trust Him with our deepest thoughts and emotions.

REFLECTION

Psalm 62:8 says "O my people, trust in Him at all times. Pour out your heart to Him, for God is our refuge." (NLT) Pouring out your heart before God is a position of complete surrender and total transparency. Examine your prayer life. Are there areas of your life which seem "off limits" when you talk to God? There is nothing we can hide from God. He knows us better than we do ourselves. He sees our true motives, and what fuels our attitudes and actions. (see Psalm 33:13-15) We have a Friend who understands our weaknesses, has the vision to see who we're created to be, and who gives us the knowledge and power to live out that divine purpose.

NOTES

BE THOU MY VISION

Lyrics by Dallan Forgaill, Eleanor Henrietta Hull;
Translated by Mary Elizabeth Byrne (1912)

Thou and thou only first in my heart,
High King of heaven, my treasure thou art ...
Still be my vision, O Ruler of all.

Read: 2 Corinthians 4

Jesus said: "Your eye is like a lamp that provides light for your body. When your eye is healthy, your whole body is filled with light. But when your eye is unhealthy, your whole body is filled with darkness. And if the light you think you have is actually darkness, how deep that darkness is!" (Matthew 6:22-23 NLT) Our vision was flooded with light when we first accepted Christ. Just as the temple veil was torn as Jesus died and reconciled all humanity to God; in that initial moment of salvation, our eyes became unveiled to the glory and truth of our Saviour. But has that light dimmed over time? Is the light in our eyes a megawatt floodlight? Or has it become as small and dim as a night light?

It is much easier to travel an unfamiliar road in daylight. We can clearly see and respond to the terrain, the road signs, and the things and people around us. In darkness we cannot easily follow a sharp turn in the road; much of what surrounds us is hidden in shadows, and we're more likely to lose our way as we miss important signposts. The trajectory of our lives is similarly unfamiliar to us. We may have an idea of where we would like to end up- loved, content, successful, and accepted- these are the desires in the heart of every person. However, we have no idea how to get there or even what our destination looks like. The Gospel is no longer hidden to us, but as we travel along in this dark world there is much to deceive and dim the light, which Christ has put in us that we may see the truth in all things. We must be vigilant in maintaining that glorious light, that we would not perceive ourselves to be filled with light, when in fact we are filled with darkness. As humans we are limited by space and time; our eyes can only see what is tangible. It is so much easier to pursue and treasure those things which fill our physical space and consume our time and energy. It is a spiritual discipline to live in light of what is not seen or felt but to "…fix our gaze on things that cannot be seen." (2 Corinthians 4:18 NLT) This is only accomplished through the work of the Holy Spirit in us- just as the truth of Christ was revealed to us by the Spirit. (See 1 Thessalonians 1:4-5) This work can only happen if we intentionally seek out the truth which will illuminate the right path and expose the many pitfalls along the road.

REFLECTION

We are to treasure God's ways so that we remain on the narrow path and arrive at the destination we intended: "Your word is a lamp to my feet and light to my path … Your laws are my treasure; they are my heart's delight." (Psalm 119:105, 111 NLT) This may seem obvious and simple, especially if we accepted Christ many years ago, but it is so crucial that we recognize our human tendency to wander. We need to take an honest inventory of our heart. Ask the Lord to show you if there are any attitudes or habits that do not align with His ways. God's word trumps societal, familial, and generational norms and we must not allow what appears "right" or "acceptable" in our culture to dilute the truth. May our prayer always be: "Turn my eyes from worthless things, and give me life through your word." (Psalm 119:37 NLT)

NOTES

BRINGING IN THE SHEAVES

Lyrics by Knowles Shaw (1874)

Sowing in the sunshine, sowing in the shadows ...
We shall come rejoicing, bringing in the sheaves

Read: Matthew 13:1-23

God calls us to labor in His field and share the Good News (see 1 Corinthians 3:9), however many of us have abdicated this calling; not out of a lack of compassion or missional focus, but out of discouragement. It certainly is disheartening to care deeply for the salvation of those around us and find that years and decades go by for some without much visible fruit.

In the parable of the sower, Jesus illustrates that a seed must be sown on fertile soil to yield fruit. Although certain terrain is inherently more fertile, anyone who has ever planted a garden or maintained a yard knows that the condition of soil can be improved by care or worsened by neglect. The footpath in the sower's field could be excavated to reveal fertile soil. The ground infested with thorns could be cleaned up and fertilized. The rocks in the shallow soil could be dug up and replaced with fertile soil. Similarly, the condition of a person's heart can change. Only God knows our heart, and in His love, He draws our heart to His. In Ezekiel 11 God speaks of the rebellious nation of Israel saying "I will give them an undivided heart and put a new spirit in them; *I will remove from them their heart of stone and give them a heart of flesh. Then they will follow my decrees and be careful to keep my laws. They will be my*

39

people, and I will be their God." (Ezekiel 11:19-20 NIV, emphasis mine) Though the Israelites' hearts could be compared to the footpath where the seed fell and was eaten by birds- dense, hard, impenetrable; God promised to change their hearts so that they would be reconciled to Him.

God can use anything- a person, a circumstance, a divine encounter; to transform a person's heart. Regardless of how fertile the soil, it will not bear fruit if there is no seed sown. That is our role. The hearts of those who understand the Gospel must work alongside the Holy Spirit to produce an abundant harvest (see Romans 10:17). We must not grow weary or complacent in planting seeds of truth and kindness in the lives of those around us. Who knows what fruit it will bear? We will rejoice on that day when the harvest is gathered and we see that the seeds we have planted in faith have not only brought life to an individual, but have multiplied and blessed many.

REFLECTION

We do not need to carry the weight of "saving" people. It is the Lord who saves, the Holy Spirit who reveals the truth of Christ to each of us (1 Thessalonians 1:4-5). We have the awesome privilege of partnering with God as sowers of the seed of the gospel. The Lord can bless a farmer with good land, ample rain, and a favorable climate, but if he or she never goes out and plants anything, there will be no harvest. We need to leave the things out of our control to Him, and faithfully do the work He has called us to do: "Let's not get tired of doing what is good. At just the right time we will reap a harvest of blessing *if we don't give up*." (Galatians 6:9 NLT, emphasis mine) Perhaps there is someone on your mind right now who you have been longing to see come to Christ. Ask God to continue to work in their heart and to give you the strength and courage to consistently show up for them so they may see God's love and hear His message.

NOTES

GREAT IS THY FAITHFULNESS

Lyrics by Thomas O. Chisholm (1923)

Great is Thy faithfulness
O God my Father
There is no shadow of turning with Thee
Thou changest not
Thy compassions they fail not
As Thou hast been
Thou forever will be

Read: Nehemiah 9:1-37

Throughout the Old Testament we observe the many victories and failures of the nation of Israel. Often it seems as if they have a hopeless case of amnesia. Despite the many signs and wonders they experienced, they habitually forsake the Lord. These are a few highlights:

One month after being miraculously freed from slavery in Egypt, the Israelites fear starvation in the wilderness and complain to Moses and Aaron saying, "If only the Lord had killed us back in Egypt." (Exodus 16:3 NLT) The Lord sends them manna from Heaven in the morning and quail in the evening. The Lord fed His people in this manner for 40 years. (Exodus 16:11-13,35)

Again, Israel grumbles against God when they approach the Promised Land. When met with the report that the land is filled with giants, they are paralyzed with fear and plot to return to Egypt. (Numbers 14:1-4) Joshua and Caleb attempt to encourage their faith: "The land we traveled through and explored is a wonderful land! And if the Lord is pleased with us, He will bring us safely into that land and give it to us ... Do not rebel against the Lord, and don't be afraid of the people of the land ... They have no protection, but the Lord is with us!" (Numbers 14:7-9 NLT) But the Israelites refuse to listen.

Joshua and his generation pass away, and the next generations forget the Lord. God raises up judges to lead Israel, however the Israelites continue to rebel: "...Israel did not listen to the judges but prostituted themselves by worshiping other gods ... Whenever the Lord raised up a judge over Israel, he was with that judge and rescued the people from their enemies throughout the judge's lifetime ... But when the judge died, the people returned to their corrupt ways, behaving worse than those who had lived before them." (Judges 2:16-19 NLT)

Israel asks the Lord for a king, and so King Saul is the first in a long succession of rulers. After King Solomon's reign the nation is divided, and the kings of both Israel and Judah often ignore God's laws and the warnings of the prophets. Many of them worship false idols and lead the people astray: "Our kings, leaders, priests, and ancestors did not obey your Law or listen to the warnings in your commands and laws. Even while they had their own kingdom, they did not serve you ..." (Nehemiah 9:34-35a NLT) Eventually the people are scattered and in exile- Israel is defeated by the Assyrians and Judah by the Babylonians.

As we read about the tumultuous history of the nation of Israel it is easy to cast judgement- what a rebellious and fickle people! But if we take a genuine look at our own histories, can we honestly claim the high ground? How many times have we turned to things and people for comfort, security, and approval rather than relying on God? How many times have we gone ahead with our own plans without consulting our Father? How often have we experienced a crisis and fallen into despair and misery rather than entrusting our cares to the Lord? Their story and our stories are then not only about failure and sin, but about the God who has kept us in His hands through it all. They deserved, and we also deserve to be tossed away; abandoned and forgotten, for what person could endure such rejection and betrayal? But our God is unrelenting in His love, "For his unfailing love for us is powerful; the Lord's faithfulness endures forever." (Psalm 117:2 NLT) When we were His enemy, He gave everything for us. (Romans 5:8) His love is boundless and unfathomable. And as we stumble and struggle through this life, he continues to lavish His love on us. We at times are inconsistent and distrusting, but our God abounds in mercy and love; great is thy faithfulness.

REFLECTION

May this be our prayer:

> "Have mercy on me, O God, because of your unfailing love. Because of your great compassion, blot out the stain of my sins … Create in me a clean heart, O God. Renew a loyal spirit within me." (Psalm 51:1,10 NLT)

We must regularly go before God in reverence and ask Him to show us our waywardness. Though most of us would not dare to bow down before images of wood and gold as the Israelites did, we must recognize that the Lord sees our heart, and we must admit that at times He does not occupy the throne. The Lord is faithful to forgive. As we come to recognize our failings, repent, and experience His mercy and kindness; our love for Him and faithfulness to Him will continue to grow.

NOTES

COME THOU FOUNT OF EVERY BLESSING

Lyrics by Robert Robinson (1758)

Come, Thou Fount of every blessing
Tune my heart to sing Thy grace
Streams of mercy, never ceasing
Call for songs of loudest praise …
Here's my heart, oh, take and seal it
Seal it for Thy courts above

Read: Psalm 40

We crave authenticity. If we think about our closest and most treasured relationships, it is with those who are vulnerable and willing to tell us the truth (even when it's not pretty). At the core of our desire for realness is a longing to know that we are not alone. We want to be seen and understood. We are called to integrity as followers of Christ, and it is beneficial to find knowledge and support in our shared experiences. However, in the pursuit of authenticity we can fall into the habit of focusing on our challenges and troubles while forgetting to pursue joy and gratefulness.

The first verse of "Come Thou Fount of Every Blessing" implores us to declare the mercy, grace, and majesty of God. The last verse, to tether our hearts to His. We see this in Psalm 40 as David affirms the power and faithfulness of God despite being surrounded by troubles (Psalm

49

40:12-17). David ultimately knows that God's heart is kind toward him, and he finds comfort and contentment in this. Although candid about his trials, he ultimately recognizes that God has been abundantly good to him: "O Lord my God, you have performed many wonders for us. Your plans for us are too numerous to list. You have no equal. If I tried to recite all your wonderful deeds, I would never come to the end of them." (Psalm 40:5 NLT) Do we recite the wonderful deeds of God, or are we rehearsing our struggles? Are our thoughts consumed by joy, reverence, love, and hope? Or do we dwell on our hardships and disappointments? Not only is suffering necessary for us to experience the miracles that will bolster our faith and draw others to Christ, but we can find joy in the midst of trials as we are drawn to the awesome presence of God and experience His supernatural grace every day.

Although we may suffer to different degrees, we all suffer. We struggle through much of this life, and admittedly it is easy to forget what is good in the midst of hardship. We may forfeit wonder and adoration for cynicism and grumbling. We must "tune" our heart to God's- recognizing that His purposes and glory are paramount. We ought to continually praise God, for He has lifted us "out of the pit of despair, out of the mud and the mire" of sin and given us an unshakable foundation in Christ (Psalm 40:2 NLT). As followers of Christ, we should be "real". Our authenticity will draw others to us as they search to be seen and understood. But let us tell the whole story- one of struggle, disappointment, and pain; but also, one of comfort, rest, and assurance. We can reject the temptation to wallow in our suffering, and instead rejoice as we look to the One who does all things well.

REFLECTION

We should share our suffering with others not only for the sake of "keeping it real", but to bring glory to our Father in Heaven. If we really know the Savior and King, we cannot bemoan our trials until we are rescued. It is in hardship and discomfort- not in spite of it, that we find blessing and joy. It is in our weakness that we are reminded of our limitations and are awed by the Creator and Sustainer of all things. It is in destitution that we experience God's provision. It is in danger that we find safety under His wings. It is in sorrow that we seek the loving embrace of our Father. There is beauty in the struggle as Christ is revealed in us:

> "In everything we do, we show that we are true ministers of God. We patiently endure troubles and hardships and calamities of every kind. We have been beaten, been put in prison, faced angry mobs, worked to exhaustion, endured sleepless nights, and gone without food. We prove ourselves by our purity, our understanding, our patience, our kindness, by the Holy Spirit within us, and by our sincere love. ... *God's power is working in us.* We serve God whether people honor us or despise us, whether they slander us or praise us. We are honest, but they call us impostors ... We live close to death, but we are still alive. We have been beaten, but we have not been killed. *Our hearts ache, but we always have joy. We are poor, but we give spiritual riches to others. We own nothing, and yet we have everything.*" (2 Corinthians 6:4-6, 8-10 NLT, emphasis mine)

NOTES

THE OLD RUGGED CROSS

Lyrics by George Bennard (1913)

And I'll cherish the old rugged Cross
Till my trophies at last I lay down
I will cling to the old rugged Cross
And exchange it some day for a crown

Read: Hebrews 11:32-40, 12:1-12

In Mark 10:17-29 (and Matthew 19 and Luke 18) a rich man approached Jesus and asked him what he must do to inherit eternal life. Jesus first quoted from the Ten Commandments, and when the man said that he had followed those commands, Jesus then told him that he must sell everything he owns, give the money to the poor, and follow Him. The man was saddened by this directive, as he had many possessions. It is interesting that when quoting the Ten Commandments, Jesus only mentioned those relating to our relationships with others and left out the other four regarding our relationship with God (see Exodus 20:3-17). These commands (you must have no other God before Me, keep the sabbath holy, you must not make for yourself or bow down before idols, and you must not misuse the name of the Lord) expose our attitude toward God; they determine if He is truly Lord over our life. The rich man lived a technically "good" life- he hadn't harmed anyone, been dishonest, or disrespectful. But his heart wasn't totally surrendered to God. He treasured his riches above the things of God.

Hebrews 11 lists the many faithful servants of God. These men and women all had different strengths, weaknesses, and experiences, but they had one thing in common- their perspective was not limited to this earth; their eyes were fixed on the Lord. Abraham left his home and lived among foreigners, for he " …was confidently looking forward to a city with eternal foundations, a city designed and built by God." (Hebrews 11:10 NLT) Moses chose God's purposes over the wealth and power of royalty: "He chose to share the oppression of God's people instead of enjoying the fleeting pleasures of sin. He thought it was better to suffer for the sake of Christ than to own the treasures of Egypt, for he was looking ahead to his great reward. It was by faith that Moses left the land of Egypt, not fearing the king's anger. He kept right on going because he kept his eyes on the one who is invisible." (Hebrews 11:25-27 NLT) These people, and all the others listed in Hebrews 11 stand in stark contrast to the rich ruler. They did not seek only to fulfill the letter of the law; understanding that honoring God should be foremost in all things. They knew that the riches found in Christ were far more glorious than anything they would possess on earth. Their faith did not emerge from wishful thinking or superhuman strength, but a love for God that eclipsed the pleasures and pain of this world.

These "heroes of the faith" were regular people, just like us, but they had unwavering confidence in God and accomplished great things in the name of the Lord, despite great opposition and suffering. When we read about their lives it is tempting to put them on a pedestal; they are people to admire but impossible to emulate. How is it that they forsook this world for a kingdom they could not see? As Jesus explained to his disciples, "Humanly speaking, it is impossible. But not with God. Everything is possible with God." (Mark 10:27 NLT)

We can easily lose focus on the One who is invisible when we are surrounded by a culture that values achievement and self-promotion. Our senses are bombarded by people and things vying for our attention. God gives us a supernatural ability to see what is not perceived with our natural eyes or felt in our flesh- to press past pleasure and pain to spend our time, energy, and money investing in His kingdom which is unshakeable (Hebrews 12:28). All the wealth, power, talent, and knowledge we accumulate in this life will come to an end. When the splendor of God's kingdom is revealed in its fulness, all that we have forfeited to follow Jesus will be restored to us in abundance (Mark 10:29-30). There is no more fulfilling and rewarding purpose than being a part of bringing the kingdom of Heaven to earth.

REFLECTION

Experiencing the miraculous and transformative power of God which enables us to seek the kingdom of heaven whilst living in this world is not done passively. We need to be intentional and persistent in our determination to cherish Christ above all else. We must "cling to the old rugged cross." To 'cling' is to hold on tightly and fervently. You cannot cling to something while holding on to a few other things; it is a dynamic, focused, and exclusive action. God's word instructs us to " ...fix our eyes on Jesus" (Hebrews 12:2, NIV). Again, this is a deliberate action. If you've ever had a staring contest with someone, you know how difficult it is to look at something without breaking focus. As we humbly and consistently ask the Lord to turn our attention away from worthless, temporary pursuits and instead toward His will and eternal glory, He will reveal the true motives of our heart and give us the desire and strength to treasure Him.

God has called His disciples to remote, impoverished, and dangerous parts of the world, but he has also called some of us to our "regular" homes, offices, schools, communities, and businesses. Our circles of influence, resources, and talents are to be vehicles which bring the kingdom of Heaven to earth; they are not for our own benefit. Let's not waste our time and energy here grasping at what is fleeting and meaningless, but rather live purposefully: "So, be careful how you live. Don't live like fools, but like those who are wise. *Make the most of every opportunity* in these evil days. *Don't act thoughtlessly, but understand what the Lord wants you to do.*" (Ephesians 5:15-17 NLT, emphasis mine)

NOTES

BREAK THOU THE BREAD OF LIFE

Lyrics by Mary A. Lathbury (1877)

Break Thou the Bread of Life,
Dear Lord, to me,
As Thou didst break the loaves
Beside the sea;
Beyond the sacred page
I seek Thee, Lord;
My spirit pants for Thee,
O Living Word

Read: John 6:22-59

Perhaps one of the most well-known miracles of Jesus is when He fed five thousand men (in addition to women and children) by the Sea of Galilee with five loaves of bread and two fish. After everyone ate and was satisfied, there was still food leftover (John 6:10-13). The people were amazed by this miraculous sign and followed Jesus the next day to the other side of shore. Despite all the miracles they had seen Jesus do (John 6:1), they still demanded a sign as proof of His identity as the Messiah (John 6:30-31). The crowd failed to understand that these signs were not meant to sustain them, but to encourage their faith so that they may turn to Him who would satisfy them completely and continually. Jesus corrects them saying:

> "I tell you the truth, Moses didn't give you bread from
> heaven. My Father did. And now he offers you the true

59

bread from heaven. The true bread of God is the one who comes down from heaven and gives life to the world ... I am the bread of life. Whoever comes to me will never be hungry again. Whoever believes in me will never be thirsty ... Your ancestors ate manna in the wilderness, but they all died. Anyone who eats the bread from heaven, however, will never die." (John 6:32-33,35, 49-50 NLT)

Not only must we be captivated by the One who does the impossible, rather than the people He may use or the miracles themselves; Jesus also reminds us that the Bread of Life is all sufficient. God did provide for the Israelites in a supernatural way, however they eventually died. This bread, though it was extraordinary, only nourished their bodies and ultimately could not save them. Jesus was calling His followers; and is calling us today to desire more. As evidenced by the crowd who followed Jesus, signs and wonders will never satisfy us. If it is only about witnessing an amazing event, we will soon need another "fix" to bolster our faith. Jesus is the Bread of Life, the Word who came down from Heaven to give us life (John 1:4,14). As such, His miracles, His word, His message are more than just something to marvel at. It has the power to transform our lives, to nourish our souls so that we may grow and be healthy. As the hymn quoted above says, let us seek the Lord "beyond the sacred page". Let the miracles we read about in His word and let the wonders we experience in our own lives draw us to the source of life. Let us read His word not simply as a spiritual discipline; let us crave the revelation that comes when we allow the words to jump off the page and be written upon our hearts. As we discover who God is and who we are, (by reading, meditating upon, and accepting His word) our thoughts, priorities, words, and actions will be transformed.

REFLECTION

As Jesus' disciples, we have accepted the Bread from Heaven. We partake of His body and blood that give us salvation and eternal life. The Bread of Life not only rescues us from the grave, but also relieves us of a life of trying to satisfy the desires of our insatiable flesh. Once we have experienced the living Word in all its richness and sweetness, why would we settle for anything less? The Lord invites us to eat and drink of Him and be satisfied: "Everyone who thirsts, come to the waters; and you who have no money come, buy grain and eat. Come, buy wine and milk without money and without cost [simply accept it as a gift from God]. *Why do you spend money for that which is not bread, and your earnings for what does not satisfy? Listen carefully to Me, and eat what is good, and let your soul delight in abundance.*" (Isaiah 55:1-2, AMP, emphasis mine)

When it comes to our physical bodies, we become desperate if we are extremely hungry or thirsty. We are sluggish, irrational, and ineffective as we become dehydrated or our blood sugar plummets. We will eat or drink just about anything to satisfy our hunger or quench our thirst. Even if a gourmet feast were set before us, we would eat it too quickly, not mindful of the quality or appreciative of its flavor. It is the same in our spiritual life. If we do not seek His life-giving bread, we will find ourselves in the fast food drive-thru of spiritual nourishment- settling for a relationship with God that is more about survival than growth. We will forget to savor the sweetness and wonder of the Lord's presence. We will miss the good things He is doing in our life each day. Why seek rest, comfort, wisdom, acceptance, joy, and love in places that have no substance and bear potentially unhealthy consequences? The Bread of

61

Life is free of cost and the best food for our souls. Why wait until we are spiritually starved to seek God and miss out on the delight of living an unburdened, abundant life? God is reminding us today to crave the Bread of Life, the only One who will truly satisfy us.

NOTES

I SURRENDER ALL

Lyrics by Judson W. Van De Venter (1896)

All to Jesus I surrender
All to Him I freely give
I will ever love and trust Him
In His presence daily live

Read: Daniel 6:1-23

Prayer is fundamentally an act of surrender. We surrender our time, our cares, our will, our pride, our flesh, and our own understanding as we commune with God. We see throughout scripture that, "The earnest prayer of a righteous person has great power and produces wonderful results." (James 5:16b NLT) At its core, prayer invites Heaven to invade the earth, for light and truth to dispel the darkness and deceit in ourselves and in this world.

Daniel recognized the power of prayer and made it a priority in his life. Prayer was not just something he did, it was ingrained in his schedule: "But when Daniel learned that the law had been signed, he went home and knelt down *as usual* in his upstairs room...He prayed three times a day, *just as he had always done,* giving thanks to his God." (Daniel 6:10 NLT, emphasis mine) For Daniel, the time he spent in prayer was not determined by how he felt or what commitments he had day-to-day; it was just a fact of life. At first glance this may seem overly religious and perhaps a habit compelled by obligation and not love. But are there not many beneficial things in life that require discipline? If we only exercised when we were "in the mood", it is unlikely we would reach our fitness goals. If we only spent quality time with our loved ones when it was convenient, our relationships would suffer. The interesting thing about discipline that we seem to forget is that desire inspires discipline, and discipline fuels desire. As we commit ourselves to something and experience the benefits, our habit grows roots- we "fall in love" with that goal, hobby, or person over and over.

If Daniel prayed three times a day only as a show of piety, he may have refrained from praying for thirty days. He would have avoided breaking the law and could have rationalized that he was not breaking God's law so long as he did not pray to anyone else. But for Daniel, this compromise was not acceptable. It was in the practice of prayer that he found the strength and courage to continue praying, even when this meant risking his life. Daniel's experience of prayer demonstrates what Jesus taught in Matthew 6. Jesus rebuked the religious leaders' shallow piety and the Gentiles' verbose petitions. Jesus reminds us that we yield our time and will to God in prayer not so that we would fulfill an obligation, but that we may experience His goodness:

> "When you pray, don't be like the hypocrites who love to pray publicly on street corners and in the synagogues where everyone can see them. I tell you the truth that is all the reward they will ever get. But when you pray, go away by yourself, shut the door behind you, and pray to your Father in private. *Then your Father, who sees everything, will reward you.* When you pray, don't babble on and on as the Gentiles do. They think their prayers are answered merely by repeating their words again and again. Don't be like them, for *your Father knows exactly what you need even before you ask him!*" (Matthew 6:5-9 NLT, emphasis mine)

The discipline of prayer is then not only a matter of religious custom, but a holy invitation to meet with our Heavenly Father. There is a great reward in this discipline where tradition meets love- the peace of knowing God's character, the wisdom of knowing His will, and the grace to do His will.

REFLECTION

What is hindering the practice of prayer in your life? Firstly, like Daniel, we must make prayer a regular part of our day. It is highly unlikely that we will maintain an active prayer life if we wait for the right circumstances. Inevitably, life's busyness and burdens will sabotage even the best of intentions. The holy fear found in worship, the rest found in His love, and the opportunity to hear His instruction are found in these quiet moments with the Lord.

Secondly, we must abandon our notion of "ideal prayer". We do not pray to impress God (or others) with our eloquence or theological know-how. We do not recite rote prayers mindlessly as a religious exercise. We do not pray to coerce the favor of God. We persist in prayer simply because we desire to know Him:

> "O God, you are my God; I earnestly search for you. My soul thirsts for you; my whole body longs for you in this parched and weary land where there is no water. I have seen you in your sanctuary and gazed upon your power and glory. Your unfailing love is better than life itself; how I praise you! I will praise you as long as I live, lifting up my hands to you in prayer." (Psalm 63:1-5a NLT)

So, what does the "right" prayer sound like? It sounds like whatever is sincere. Whether that is a joyful song, a lamenting cry, a posture of repentance, or a contemplative conversation; it is all done from a heart that wants Him above all else.

As we commit today to make prayer a priority in our lives, we do so out of genuine love for our Savior. As we fulfill our commitment, this love will grow and sustain our habit of prayer. Surrender begets surrender- a beautiful cycle of devotion.

NOTES

ABIDE WITH ME

Lyrics by Henry Francis Lyte (1847)

I need Thy presence every passing hour:
What but Thy grace can foil the tempter's power?
Who like Thyself my guide and stay can be?
Through cloud and sunshine, oh, abide with me.

Read: John 14:16-31

As followers of Christ, when we go through trials, we may retreat into fear and gloom for a time, but eventually (and as we grow in our faith, immediately) we seek the Lord's comfort, strength, and guidance. In these times when we are met with circumstances which threaten to destroy us, we cry out to the Lord, and others also intercede for us. We cling to Him, we crave His presence and long to hear His voice.

However, when we are not in crisis, it is tempting to forget that we are in fact still facing a battle. If we belong to Christ, we are being relentlessly pursued by an enemy who desires to distract, deceive, torment, ruin, and ultimately kill us. Whether we are in difficult circumstances or we're in an "uneventful" season of life, there is an unseen fight not only around us, but against us. (Ephesians 6:12) The Lord has instructed us to be aware of our enemy (1 Peter 5:8). Acknowledging our enemy does not give Satan authority in our lives, but rather the contrary. Jesus knew who His adversary was and called him out by name. Jesus recognized that He was not contending with the religious rulers who sentenced Him to death- He was wrestling with the same enemy who seeks our destruction: "I will not speak with you much longer, for the ruler of the world (Satan) is coming. And *he has no claim on Me [no power over Me nor anything that he can use against Me]*; but so that the world may know [without any doubt] that I love the Father, I do exactly as the Father has commanded Me [and act in full agreement with Him]." (John 14:30-31, AMP, emphasis mine) Our Savior did not ignore or water down Satan's power or intention, and we also cannot go about our lives spiritually unconscious until a crisis demands our attention. The simplest battle to win is against an opponent who is easily ambushed by their enemy. On the other hand, Jesus has not called us to cower in fear and be constantly frustrated by the schemes of Satan. The acknowledgement of our foe should not paralyze us in anxiety and despair, but rather ready us for the fight. We will be ready to fight and win because just as Jesus declared that Satan had no power over Him, we also know that we who are in Christ are victorious over our enemy.

So, we know who our adversary is, and we know we can triumph over him- but how is this accomplished? Our God has given us an unseen weapon to win this unseen fight. When we accepted the message of the Gospel, we received the gift of the Holy Spirit, just as Jesus promised. (Ephesians 1:13). Jesus describes the role of the Spirit in our lives- He is the one who enables us to be alert, wise, and strong: "But the Helper (Comforter, Advocate, Intercessor—Counselor, Strengthener, Standby), the Holy Spirit, whom the Father will send in My name, He will teach you all things. And He will help you remember everything that I have told you." (John 14:26, AMP) Satan has already lost the war. Jesus has overcome sin and the grave, and death also has no power over us as children of God. Our enemy may not succeed in dragging us back into the kingdom of darkness, however, if we deny the work of the Holy Spirit in our lives, he will very easily be able to make us ineffective witnesses to the Gospel and rob us of our divine purpose. We need to invite the Holy Spirit to abide with us every moment of each day so that we will see the enemy's attack coming from a mile away. We will not be caught unaware, and we will not be destroyed in even the fiercest battle as we follow the leading of the Spirit of God.

REFLECTION

We all have our weaknesses. When put under pressure, there are facets of our personality which will manifest attitudes and behaviours that do not align with God's ways. Sometimes it seems we cannot help ourselves; even though in retrospect we may recognize that we handled a situation poorly, in the moment we act instinctively. Our enemy is aware of where we are vulnerable. He is not arbitrarily attacking us; he is scheming against us. We cannot live in autopilot, only seeking God's presence when our circumstances are desperate. If we are going to win the battle and live purposeful, effective, and abundant lives, we should strive to be proactive rather than reactive:

> "But I say, walk *habitually* in the [Holy] Spirit [*seek Him and be responsive to His guidance*], and then you will certainly not carry out the desire of the sinful nature [*which responds impulsively* without regard for God and His precepts] … If we [claim to] live by the [Holy] Spirit, we must also walk by the Spirit [with personal integrity, godly character, and moral courage—*our conduct empowered by the Holy Spirit*]." (Galatians 5:16,25, AMP, emphasis mine)

With the Holy Spirit as our guide, our personality will be shaped not by our history, but by the life-transforming power of God. Our unhealthy and sinful habits will be replaced by beneficial and righteous habits. We will be an example of love, hope, faith, and peace to those around us and fight on behalf of those God has placed in our path, so that they too would experience the victory found only in Christ.

NOTES

BE STILL MY SOUL

Lyrics by Kathrina von Schlegel,
Translated by Jane Borthwick (1855)

Be still my soul the Lord is on thy side
Bear patiently the cross of grief or pain
Leave to thy God to order and provide
In every change He faithful will remain
Be still my soul thy best, thy heavenly friend
Through thorny ways leads to a joyful end

Read: Isaiah 40:12-31

God speaks through the prophet Isaiah and reminds His people that He is the one true God. He is not a god created; He is the Creator. He is not bound by space or time. He is all powerful; the ultimate source of wisdom and understanding: "Who else has held the oceans in his hand? Who has measured off the heavens with his fingers? Who else knows the weight of the earth or has weighed the mountains and hills on a scale? Who is able to advise the Spirit of the Lord?" (Isaiah 40:12-13 NLT) It is only the Lord who has the power and wisdom to heal, provide, and bring order where there is chaos.

Our God is to be feared for His sovereignty and holiness, but also for his fierce love and kindness. In Isaiah 40:21-27, the prophet reminds us that God is mindful of all His creation: "O Jacob, how can you say the Lord does not see your troubles? O Israel, how can you say God ignores your rights?" (Isaiah 40:27 NLT) He has named each of the stars. He cares for the birds and the flowers (Matthew 6:26-30). He created us and knew us before we were born (Psalm 139:13-16). God does nothing haphazardly; He is intimately involved in every detail of our lives. There is no question that "the Lord is on thy side". He has proven His nature from the beginning of time. We can be still- free from turmoil in the presence of a holy and loving God.

Isaiah 40 ends in a familiar passage: "But those who wait for the Lord [who expect, look for, and hope in Him] will gain new strength and renew their power; they will lift up their wings [and rise up close to God] like eagles; they will run and not become weary, they will walk and not grow tired." (Isaiah 40:31 AMP) We will continually find strength as we trust and rely upon God, whether in a season of running or walking.

Perhaps you are moving swiftly toward a destination- running toward a dream, embarking on a new venture. Things are moving quickly, the pressure is demanding, and it may feel like there is no time to hesitate or rest. Or maybe you have experienced tremendous loss and you are in the thick of grief. You are overwhelmed and struggling to push forward. God promises that if you put your hope in Him, you will have supernatural strength and incomprehensible peace (Philippians 4:6-7). It is when life gets difficult that we may neglect consistently seeking the Lord and meeting with other believers. We may feel we don't have time or energy for these spiritual disciplines, but actually we don't have time *not* to seek God. As you are still before the Lord, you will have the vigor to meet many challenges, you will have wisdom for every situation, and you will do more and go further than you could in your own strength.

For some, you are in a season of walking. Life may feel a bit mundane; maybe you have hopes and dreams that seem far off and aren't really your focus right now. Or maybe you have just achieved a milestone and are at a plateau. It is tempting in these times to lose sight of the larger picture. It is easy to wander off the right path if we feel we aren't headed anywhere meaningful or profound. These parts of life require consistency and focus. The Lord is with those who are steadfast: "The eyes of the Lord search the whole earth in order to strengthen those whose hearts are fully committed to him." (2 Chronicles 16:9 NLT, emphasis mine) As we wait on the Lord, we will not lose heart and meander off course or set up camp on the side of the road, abandoning our calling. We will find purpose in the mundane and "insignificant"; we will see the joy and promise in "small" victories.

REFLECTION

When faced with a crisis, with suffering, with disappointment, or with overwhelm, we are often either too quick to spring into action or are paralyzed by the weight of life's challenges. We make short-sighted and unwise decisions, we speak careless words, we seek help in questionable places. The Lord reminds His people through the prophet Isaiah, and He is reminding us today that it is in stillness that there is strength: "Only in returning to me and resting in me will you be saved. *In quietness and confidence is your strength* ... So the Lord must wait for you to come to him so he can show you his love and compassion. For the Lord is a faithful God." (Isaiah 30:15,18 NLT, emphasis mine)

NOTES

TAKE MY LIFE AND LET IT BE

Lyrics by Frances Ridley Havergal (1874)

Take my life and let it be consecrated,
Lord, to thee ...
Take my heart it is thine own;
it shall be thy royal throne

Read: Daniel 3

Shadrach, Meshach, and Abednego were foreigners in Babylon. They had been separated from their families, culture, and emblems of faith (Daniel 1:1-6). It would have been easy for them to adopt the Babylonian way of life (they had spent several years being taught their history and values), but we see in Daniel chapter 1 that from the outset they set themselves apart, holding tightly to their Jewish heritage. When we meet them again in Daniel chapter 3, it is clear that despite their learning and despite the time they had spent immersed in the Babylonian culture, they remained uncorrupted, maintaining their fear of the One true God. When threatened with death for their persistence in remaining faithful to the Lord, they reply, "O Nebuchadnezzar, *we do not need to defend ourselves before you. If we are thrown into the blazing furnace, the God whom we serve is able to save us.* He will rescue us from your power, Your Majesty. *But even if he doesn't, we want to make it clear to you, Your Majesty, that we will never serve your gods or worship the gold statue you have set up.*" (Daniel 3:16-18 NLT, emphasis mine) Their response demonstrates that they know who their God is- all powerful, and attentive to the needs of His children; and consequently, they know who they are- faithful servants of the Lord. Their answer to the king's decree is unwavering and unapologetic. They are fully convinced of who their King is and where their allegiance lies.

Much like these three godly young men, we are immersed in a society that doesn't always align with our identity as children of God. We are pulled in a thousand directions- contradictory and ever-changing ideas competing for our approval. We are accused of being intolerant, judgemental, and narrow minded. The word of God is misused by some to endorse unhealthy and immoral actions, and by others to incite hatred and fear. What are we to do with all this noise? We should not be offended or discouraged by our discomfort in this world, in fact, we ought to be uneasy living on this earth. If we are untroubled by and loved by this world, we do not belong to Him:

> "I told them many things while I was with them in this world so they would be filled with my joy. I have given them your word. And the world hates them because they do not belong to the world, just as I do not belong to the world. I'm not asking you to take them out of the world, but to keep them safe from the evil one. They do not belong to this world any more than I do. Make them holy by your truth; teach them your word, which is truth. Just as you sent me into the world, I am sending them into the world. And I give myself as a holy sacrifice for them so they can be made holy by your truth." (John 17:13-19 NLT)

Jesus prays this over His disciples before He goes to the cross. This prayer is also for us today as His children. We are "filled with joy" in spite of our discomfort and trials in this world because we know to whom we belong, and ultimately, where we belong. As we live holy, uncompromising, unashamed lives, we point to Jesus.

REFLECTION

God could have rescued Shadrach, Meshach, and Abednego from Babylon's raid of Jerusalem. They could have been passed over for a position in the royal service, and perhaps no one would have taken notice of them. But God wants the world to take notice of His people. We are here to stand out, to live righteously and with hope in a world filled with corruption and fear.

What do you stand for? Are you aware of what is happening in your community, country, and the world? Have you allowed your values and priorities to be tainted by the culture you live in? Do you avoid situations that have the potential to be inconvenient or challenging?

We can be neither ignorant, compromising, nor silent. When we accepted Christ, we became His ambassadors on this earth. We do not have the option of being disengaged or lukewarm. If we truly believe He is who He says He is, and if we know that we are His children, we must be compelled to godly action:

> "What is the benefit, my fellow believers, if someone claims to have faith but has no [good] works [as evidence]? Can that [kind of] faith save him? [No, a mere claim of faith is not sufficient—genuine faith produces good works.] ... Was our father Abraham not [shown to be] justified by works [of obedience which expressed his faith] when he offered Isaac his son on the altar [as a sacrifice to God]? *You see that [his] faith was working together with his works, and as a result of the works, his faith was completed [reaching its maturity when he expressed his*

faith through obedience] ... You see that a man (believer) is justified by works and not by faith alone [that is, *by acts of obedience a born-again believer reveals his faith].*" (James 2:20-22,24 AMP, emphasis mine)

Ask the Lord for grace and courage; that the conviction in your heart would be demonstrated in your words and actions.

NOTES

WHEN I SURVEY THE WONDROUS CROSS

Lyrics by Isaac Watts (1707)

Love so amazing, so divine
Demands my soul, my life, my all

Read: 1 John 4:7-20

The love of God is something that our human intellect will never quite be able to grasp in its fullness, however we glimpse its beauty in the fact that our Lord left Heaven and came to earth. We know He loves us because He died a brutal death so that we could be reconciled to God- we could become sons and daughters of the Father we had rejected: "See what an incredible quality of love the Father has shown to us, that we would [be permitted to] be named and called and counted the children of God! And so we are!" (1 John 3:1 AMP) Spend a few moments just taking that in. If you have any doubt in your mind that you are loved by God; if you have lost your awe of the cross somewhere along the way, take a minute and meditate on this- Jesus died for you. Christ took all the guilt and shame of your sins upon Himself so that you could be blameless and know Him in this life and the life to come. God's love truly defies all logic; His actions are the epitome of sacrifice.

The word "love" gets tossed around a lot; describing our affection for both the trivial and the precious. We love tacos. We love jazz music. We love our work. We love our home. We love our friends. We love our family. We love Jesus. We understand that all these statements are not equal- we would not die for a taco, but we might die for a friend. These sentiments imply that love can be quantified; that there is a sliding scale on which we can place the things and people we love. If we look at Jesus as our example, this kind of love is not love at all: " Love bears all things [regardless of what comes], believes all things [looking for the best in each one], hopes all things [remaining steadfast during difficult times], endures all things [without weakening]. Love never fails [it never fades nor ends]." (1 Corinthians 13:7-8 AMP) Love is all in, or it is not love at all.

"We love each other because he loved us first." (1 John 4:19 NLT) We know perfect love because of our Lord and Savior- forgiving, sacrificing, and unwavering love. What right do we have to withhold this from others? Christ died for all- there are no levels to His love- it just is. Our human nature is to compartmentalize; we put exceptions, limits, and conditions on our affections. We must set these aside and embrace generosity, persistence, and self-sacrifice. Let us strive to live out true love as Jesus has truly loved us.

REFLECTION

"Dear friends, let us continue to love one another, for love comes from God. Anyone who loves is a child of God and knows God. But anyone who does not love does not know God, for God is love." (1 John 4:7-8 NLT) This verse is quite sobering. If we are honest with ourselves, do we always demonstrate the love of God? Are we willing to be inconvenienced by strangers? Do we give generously to anyone in need? Are we kind and humble in our interactions with others? Will we believe the best of and extend patience and forgiveness to our brothers and sisters in Christ? How do we treat the people closest to us; do we take them for granted, or do we honor them with our words and actions?

We are all in progress as we become more like Jesus. May we be open to His work in us. May our awe of the wondrous cross propel our commitment to truly loving others.

NOTES

AND SHOULD IT BE THAT
I SHOULD GAIN

Lyrics by Charles Wesley (1738)

My chains fell off, my heart was free;
I rose, went forth and followed Thee.
Amazing love! how can it be
That Thou, my God, should die for me?

Read: Romans 7:14-8:15

We all experience what Paul describes in Romans 7:15. We love God, we want to do what is right, but we find ourselves making poor choices; gratifying the impatience and pride of our flesh. This nature which all of humanity inherited from Adam and Eve is inherently opposed to godliness. Our natural heritage is one of bondage- we are born in chains, children of slaves:

> "I have discovered this principle of life—that when I want to do what is right, I inevitably do what is wrong ... there is another power within me that is at war with my mind. This power makes me a slave to the sin that is still within me. Oh, what a miserable person I am! Who will free me from this life that is dominated by sin and death? Thank God! The answer is in Jesus Christ our Lord." (Romans 7:21-25a NLT)

We know that Christ came and rescued us from the chains of sin, He has given us a new inheritance- one of abundance, peace, joy, and life everlasting. It is truly miraculous that our nature can be reversed- we were once the offspring of slaves and prisoners, but now we are children of the King.

But what will we do with this new heritage? We have a royal identity, however if we have not taken hold of our inheritance, we may as well still be slaves: "Think of it this way. If a father dies and leaves an inheritance for his young children, those children are not much better off than slaves until they grow up, *even though they actually own everything their father had...* And that's the way it was with us before Christ came." (Galatians 4:1-3 NLT, emphasis mine). If we have accepted Christ, the life-giving Spirit of God lives in us (Romans 8:15). The Spirit leads us into salvation and victory, but the flesh leads us to misery and ultimately, death. If we do not accept our new inheritance and continue to be led by our sinful nature, it is as if we have access to riches but choose to be destitute; we are of noble birth but choose to labor as slaves. "And Should It Be That I Should Gain" describes our desperate condition and the glorious rescue of our Saviour. Jesus has come and rescued us; He has opened the prison door. We are free! Will we declare, "I rose, went forth and followed Thee", or will we remain in the dungeon? Christ has saved us, but we must get up, shake off our chains, and walk into freedom.

REFLECTION

We may be enslaved to the expectations and opinions of others, our insecurities, the shame of our past, an addiction, or negative familial patterns. In order to break free, we must first know who we are. We must have our minds re-wired so that we shed these labels of slavery and destruction and take our rightful place as children of God. This is not pride, as our identity has been purchased by Christ's blood and not by our own merit. If we are slaves, we have a duty to fulfill the desires of our owner. But you now belong to Christ, therefore you have "no obligation" to your sinful nature. (Romans 8:12) Ask God for a revelation of your true identity as you read His word. In addition to Romans 8, these are some scriptures which will affirm your identity in Christ: John 1:12, 2 Corinthians 5:17, Galatians 3:26-29, Colossians 3:1-4, 1 Peter 2:4-10.

If we know to whom we belong, we are to live as such in the family of God. We must choose to live by the Spirit. As the battle rages within your mind, you must put the Lord in His rightful place, for "people are slaves to whatever has mastered them." (2 Peter 2:19 NIV) Our actions and habits are conceived in our mind, thus "letting your sinful nature control your mind leads to death. But letting the Spirit control your mind leads to life and peace." (Romans 8:6 NLT) The fight for our mind is only won as we steep ourselves in the transformative power of God's word. We cannot expect to win this battle if we are half-hearted in our pursuit of God and the study of His word. As we let the truth of His word renew our minds, we will be freed from everything that hinders His presence and purpose in our lives: "You will know the truth, and the truth will set you free." (John 8:32 NIV) Let us continue to pursue the truth in all things so that we may have freedom in every way.

NOTES

CROWN HIM WITH MANY CROWNS

Lyrics by Matthew Bridges (1851)

Crown him with many crowns,
the Lamb upon his throne.
Hark! how the heavenly anthem drowns
all music but its own.
Awake, my soul, and sing
of him who died for thee,
and hail him as thy matchless king
through all eternity.

Read: Psalm 107:1-32

Psalm 107 beautifully declares the redemptive work of the Lord. We as His children have experienced His wondrous deeds and continue to see His power unfold in our lives. The four circumstances described in verses 4 to 32 each reveal a facet of the Lord's work in us. Which story resonates most with you?

Perhaps you longed for belonging. You experienced abandonment, you felt rootless, rejected, and lost. The Lord has called us His own, He has given us an eternal home in Heaven and a family of believers. You were drawn to the Savior who accepted you: "I will show love to those I called 'Not loved.' And to those I called 'Not my people,' I will say, 'Now you are my people.' And they will reply, 'You are our God!'" (Hosea

2:23b NLT) The desire to belong is universal, but those of us who have especially deep wounds of betrayal and loneliness have found healing in the arms of a loving Father.

We are all rescued from spiritual bondage through Jesus. Maybe you have also been imprisoned mentally, relationally, physically, or economically. Some of us know what it is to be hopelessly tethered to a destructive person, habit, or mindset. We have been released from a pit of despair and liberated to dance in glorious light: "I will say to the prisoners, 'Come out in freedom,' and to those in darkness, 'Come into the light.' They will be my sheep, grazing in green pastures and on hills that were previously bare." (Isaiah 49:9 NLT) We who lived in chains are drawn to Christ's message of deliverance – the gospel brings light and lightness to our world, which was once dark and oppressive.

All of us were deceived, living in sin. Our lives were captained by the lies of the enemy. We were blind to our waywardness and enemies of the truth. Perhaps you can recall a specific deception, a lie you once clung to. We are grateful to have met Jesus- the Truth who rescues us from our rebellion: "And you will know the truth, and the truth will set you free … I tell you the truth, everyone who sins is a slave of sin … So if the Son sets you free, you are truly free." (John 8:32,34,36 NLT) We are now able to discern falsehood and avoid the snares of the enemy. We declare the truth in a world enslaved by deceit.

We have experienced the peace that comes only through Christ. In the tumult, He gives us rest. Do you remember a situation in your life that seemed destined for destruction? He has re-written your destiny; once we were ruled by fear, but now we have a firm foundation: "He alone is my rock and my salvation, my defense and my strong tower; I will not be shaken or disheartened." (Psalm 62:2 AMP) The Lord continues to strengthen us, shelter us, and provide everything we need even in the most difficult seasons of life.

How have you experienced the love of God? Take a moment to reflect. Let your story inspire adoration and worship. Let it encourage your heart.

Psalm 107:2 says, "Has the Lord redeemed you? Then speak out! Tell others he has redeemed you from your enemies." As your story fills you with wonder and joy, so it should for those around you. Our redemption is not only for our benefit, but for the edification of our brothers and sisters in Christ and as a light to those still in darkness. Let us give glory to God not only in our hearts, but with our mouths and with our whole lives.

REFLECTION

How are you testifying to the goodness of God? The path you have travelled is filled with grace and glory; so that Christ would be revealed: "For we are His workmanship [His own master work, a work of art], created in Christ Jesus [reborn from above—*spiritually transformed, renewed, ready to be used*] for good works, which God prepared [for us] beforehand [taking paths which He set], so that we would walk in them [*living the good life which He prearranged and made ready for us*]." (Ephesians 2:10 AMP, emphasis mine)

Ask the Lord how you can be more intentional about sharing your story. Consider the specifics of what He has done for you, so that when the opportunity arises, you will be ready with a response. Ask the Lord for courage and peace. He has ordained your journey for His glory.

NOTES

HOW DEEP THE FATHER'S LOVE FOR US

Lyrics by Stuart Townend (1995)

How deep the Father's love for us
How vast beyond all measure
That He should give His only Son
To make a wretch His treasure

Read: Luke 15:11-31

We love a good "prodigal" story. We love those stories of rescue, freedom, and healing which remind us that truly there is no one too far from God to be saved. We rejoice with those who were lost and have been found in Christ; and we are inspired to go out and preach the gospel that many more would come to know Him. But where do we find ourselves in the story of the prodigal son? The obvious answer- we remember His loving embrace when we came to our senses and received the gift of salvation. But perhaps this familiar parable is more than a depiction of the sinner lost and found- it is the story of God's power to restore each of us daily by His love.

We all have prodigal moments; times when we wander away from God, searching for pleasure, success, comfort, answers. Our leaving may not be as blatant as the son's actions in Jesus' parable; in fact, that is what makes it seem so innocent- a little compromise here and there until sin creeps into our lives: "Temptation comes from our own desires, *which entice us and drag us away. These desires give birth to sinful actions. And* when sin is allowed to grow, it gives birth to death." (James 1:14-15 NLT, emphasis mine) Now that we know Christ, we do not intentionally rebel against the will of our Father, but admittedly, to some degree or another, we miss the mark. If we are regularly reading the Word of God and are open to His correction, He will show us the error of our ways so that we can return to Him before sin's roots are established. However, if we continue to wander off, eventually we will find ourselves miles from our Father's house eating pig feed and wonder, how did I get here? We have a choice then, do we allow ourselves to be consumed by shame and fear, distancing ourselves further from the Lord? Or do we make the journey back to Him? We know that God's love never fails, and we celebrate the power of that love as we observe it in the lives of others, but somehow when it comes to our own shameful moments, we are often crippled by guilt. We are unable to move past "I am no longer worthy of being called your son." (Luke 15:19 NLT) Like the father in this parable, our Heavenly Father is earnestly waiting for us to return, ready to receive us in His love:

> "Since he did not spare even his own Son but gave him up for us all, won't he also give us everything else? Who dares accuse us whom God has chosen for his own? No one—for God himself has given us right standing with himself. Who then will condemn us? No one—for Christ Jesus died for us and was raised to life for us, and he is sitting in the place of honor at God's right hand, pleading for us. Can anything ever separate us from Christ's love? … nothing in all creation will ever be able to separate us from the love of God that is revealed in Christ Jesus our Lord." (Romans 8:32-35a, 39b NLT)

The Father's love and the Son's sacrifice has reconciled us to God. What God first intended for us has been restored- humanity in intimate communion with Him. This in itself is a wonderful mystery and demonstrates His great love for us. But the awesome thing is, He doesn't stop there- we are daily pursued by His love. He never stops desiring us, never gives up on us; no matter how many times we return- whether from a few feet off or a thousand miles away.

REFLECTION

His love is an invitation to respond in growth and maturity; to become the person He created you to be. If our hearts are pure before Him, we do not sin willfully, but dying to our flesh is a gradual process of failures and victories. Continually ask the Lord to search your heart. What thoughts have you allowed yourself to dwell on that are untruthful and unhealthy? Do you harbor bitterness toward anyone? What little habits have you let creep into your day that have the potential to become problematic? Have you (however subtly) bought into the lie that your comfort and happiness is most important?

These questions are not meant to shame you. The Lord's rebuke is not meant to crush you, but rather to lift you up:

> "And have you forgotten the encouraging words God spoke to you as his children? He said, 'My child, don't make light of the Lord's discipline, and *don't give up when he corrects you. For the Lord disciplines those he loves...*As you endure this divine discipline, remember that God is treating you as his own children...If God doesn't discipline you as he does all of his children, it means that you are illegitimate and are not really his children at all...No discipline is enjoyable while it is happening—it's painful! But afterward *there will be a peaceful harvest of right living for those who are trained in this way.*" (Hebrews 12:5-8, 11 NLT, emphasis mine)

We should be comforted by His voice that calls and instructs us, for we know that our right-standing before the Father is because of what Christ has done. He treasures us, though we are wretched. Do not allow the enemy to rob you of your position as a child of God, do not allow Satan to convince you that you're too far gone to return. Nothing and no one is too broken for God to restore. He is waiting for you to come home.

NOTES